प्रवाह..The Flow

प्रवाह..The Flow

Sampada Karlekar

Made with ❤ on the BookLeaf Publishing Platform
www.bookleafpub.in
www.bookleafpub.com

Dedication

Dedicated to that Lord...and his blessings which gave life to my words!

..Sampada

Preface

प्रवाह..The Flow...
Whatever emerged from the ocean of the mind, sometimes from the mountain of the mind, sometimes from the core of the mind, flowed straight on to the paper.
The flow must continue continuously.. because if it is stopped it will be forgotten.. and when it starts again, it will have to flow with some other current.. so it must continue..
From fantasy to reality..

From imagination to creation...
From sunrise to sunset and..
from sunset back to sunrise !!!

Acknowledgements

In the ocean of words.. feelings.. emotions..and expressions..
I am sailing with my small vessel of a creation..

They say.. ships are meant for sailing in the sea..and not for staying steady on the ports..

I am grateful for everyone who inspired me..sailing in the ocean..

First and foremost.. the one who created this Ship..
All those who ignited and fueled the ship from time to time..
Renovated and decorated it occasionally..

I am grateful for the ports..who provide shelters during stormy nights..

*I am grateful for the beaches.. who cuddled it by
their warm Sands..*

*And I know they will always be there whenever
I need them most..
With their helping hands...*

*A BIG THANK YOU AND LOVE
TO MY DEAR FAMILY AND
FRIENDS!!!
SAMPADA...*

1. The Vehicle

Sometimes enjoy cycling
leisurely..
On small pathways and
alongside the river merrily..
But at times change the gear to
reach timely...

Sometimes drive the car..
through slopes and meadows..
through sun n rains..
through mists n darks..

But ready with lights and
brakes...

Sometimes are meant for a bike..
Through twists n turns of life..
to indulge in rains n blossom in
fresh air
but ready with an art of
balancing...

Sometimes slow down the pace..
integrate yourself to nature in
grace..
walk on the white sand n green
grass..

but ready with the music of

silence..

Sometimes are for a leap in the

sky..

and have panoramic view from

the high..

discover n fly into new galaxies..

but touch the land in time from

fantasies !!

-Sampada

2. पत्ता एक गिरा

पत्ता एक गिरा.. भूमी पर पाया
कुछ ने कहा, आखिर गिर ही गया

कुछ ने देखा, क्या लहराता हुआ आया
धरती से मिला.. इतने वर्ष देकर छाया

कुछ को इसने, विनम्रता का पाठ
सिखाया
गिरते गिरते एक चींटी को भी जमीन पर
ले आया

कुछ देर पंछियों ने भी उसका साथ दिया
उसे गिरते देखकर कुछ याद आया..
कभी इस पर ही तो हमने.. जमघट था
बनाया

उसी पेड़ का एक फूल बोला..
यही तो मुझे इस जहां में लाया
फिर क्यों मुझे भी नहीं गिराया?

तो फल बोला, तेरा समय अभी नहीं
आया
देख.. यह गिरा, तो दूसरा नया आया
यह गिरा भी तो ऐसा गिरा... की खाद बन
गया
-संपदा

3. Within you...

Extract from the gold mine
within you.. though abundant..
take little by little..

To glow in the darkest time..
To flaunt in the happiest time..

To dazzle when bursting with
pride..
To survive in the rising tide..

To twinkle as the star in the sky..
To shine as a tear in eye..

To glitter on the leaf as dew
drop..
To sparkle as snow on the rock..

To keep the flame of..
your passion ignited all the time..

extract from the gold mine..
though abundant..
take little by little..
take little by little..
-Sampada

4. साहिल

खड़ी थी साहिल पर ,एक दिन यूं ही ..
दूर-दूर की लहरों को, देखती मैं रही..
बड़ी-बड़ी लहरों को देख, थम गई वही..
लहरें तो निरंतर आती ही रही

एक बड़ी लहर, साहिल तक आते-आते
छोटी हो गई..
एक - एक बूंद से ही आखिर वह थी
बनी..
वक्त के समंदर में लहरें आती ही गई..

लेकिन मैं उन लहरों को साहिल देती
गई..

कुछ पुरानी यादें साहिल पर छोड़ कर
गई
कुछ रेत के घरों को अपने साथ लेकर
गई
उन घरों के निशान मगर बाकी है अभी
वही यादें.. उन्हें बसाएंगी कभी

आज दौर ऐसा आ गया है,
कि जिंदगी को समंदर की नहीं साहिल
की जरूरत है !

-संपदा

5. Him and Her

Him and Her

"Him" and Her"..
though different from each other
are found together..
want to know.. the secret
further..?
The opposites attract each
other..

which gives the relation a honey

texture..

a continuous flow of thoughts

n ideas

towards each other..

Sometimes..

given by "Him" and taken by

"Her"

expressed by "Her" and

understood by "Him"

unsaid by "Him" and felt by

"Her"

letting go by "Her" and caught

by "Him"..

*by understanding the
misunderstandings between
"Him" and "Her"..
they weave a perfect comforter..
which covers them through life's
autumn 'n winter !!*

-Sampada

6. इंद्रधनुष

इंद्रधनुष

बैठी जो नीचे.. यादों के आसमान के..
अनगिनत.. छोटे-छोटे लम्हे बरसने लगे..
तुम्हारे साथ गुजारे हुए पलों के..

कुछ को समेट पाई अपने हाथों में..
कुछ को नहीं..

चाहती थी तुम्हें भी भीगाना..
इन हसीन यादों की बरसात में..

सोचती थी इन लम्हों की बूंदो को..
कैसे ले जाऊं अपने हाथों में..

आज अचानक इन पर जो धूप पड़ी..
तो यह इंद्रधनुष ही लाई हूं..
तुम्हारे लिए..

-संपदा

7. Eternal and Everlasting...

Eternal and Everlasting...

At this twist and turn of life...
Let's together decorate
the old world again..

Give new shape to your dreams..
And new directions to your
hopes..

Let's relive the past..while
searching for something pristine..
from the old caste..Let's grind
something new..

Light up the old paths..And
gather old friends..

recreate the old times, by the
same classic friendship formula..

Let's relinquish the illusive
modernity and take a leap in the
sky..
keeping morality at high..

Then will we witness real
prosperity..
Eternal and Everlasting....

-Sampada

8. The house is calling

The house is calling.. to become a
home..
come here..
to take a bath in the sun rays
coming from the dome..

Take your favorite book and
relax..
Or indulge in colorful memories
and flashbacks..

*Welcome to the private corner of
your own..*
To chit chat with yourself alone

*Surprise your dear ones
sometimes..*
*As they are waiting for your free
times..*

*Light candles or dress up an
empty wall..*
*The family carnival ...they will
recall..*

*Into the hustle and bustle of the
time zone..
Remember..
The house is calling to become a
home
The house is calling.. to become a
home..*
-Sampada

9. Engagement band

Engagement band

This is not just a band.. but a bond..

wherever you go..whatever you do..
whichever situation you face,
good or bad..
because..

this is not just a band.. but a bond..

You will be entangled by this cord..
this is beyond than, just an accord..
because..
this is not just a band.. but a bond..

It will unite with the period of time..
it will change its form every time..

but the magic will never fade of
this wand
because..
this is not just a band.. but a
bond

When the time requires a child in
you..
or a mature you..
this bond will sign a treaty with
you..

when the time requires courage
in you..
or compassion in you..

laughter or tantrum in you..
this will give you a free hand..
because..
this is not just a band.. but a
bond..

All that you desire..
will be bestowed upon you by
God..
because this is not just a band..
but a bond..

-Sampada

10. कविता

कविता..

कहां से आती है यह कविता..

कागज के अक्षर, है जैसे शरीर..
भावना और अर्थ है उनकी आत्मा..

उमड़ आती है यह भावना..
कभी छुटपन के आंगन से..
तो कभी यौवन के रंगों से..
या बुजुर्गी के तजुर्बे से..

तैर कर आते हैं यह अर्थ..
कभी मन के झरने से..
तो कभी मन के सागर से..
या मन के पहाड़ से

बरसते है यह धरती पर.. बरसात के साथ
उतरते हैं कभी यह धूप के साथ..
चमकते हैं कभी चांदनी के साथ..

छुप जाते हैं यह कभी रात के अंधियारे
में
फिर से लेते हैं रूप शब्दों का दिन के
उजियारे में..

बंध जाती हैं फ़िर शब्द और अर्थ की एक
रचना..
वहीं से आती है यह कविता..
वहीं से आती है यह कविता..

-संपदा

11. A Woman

Like a river..
originating from a huge
mountain..
small in the beginning but..
equally charming..
then sheltering the small
streams..
so..broadening and growing day
by day....

Whether on the way.. meets a
straight plateau or..
big rocks or boulders...yet..
prolonging the flow..

sometimes flowing through the
green forest..
sometimes falling from a high
cliff..
still upswinging..

sometimes heavy rain or..
other times the bright sunshine..

more glistening and sparkling in
that sun..
still calming him too..

but after many twists and turns..
merging into the ocean..
Converging.. and mingling..
yet standing out with self
existence
such as a woman..
a woman.. who is like the flow of
a river...
-Sampada

12. Happiness vs Peace

Long long ago.. there was a fight

between..

two states of mind..

Happiness vs Peace??

Who is elite was the question to

find..

Happiness argued.. I am quick to

achieve..

Peace responded.. I am deep and

long term..

though quick.. you are random

and short term..

*Happiness shouted..I take the
mind to the outward world...*

*Peace replied.. I turn the mind to
inward thoughts..*

*Happiness countered, I connect
all, with exteriors.*

*peace said, with a gentle smile..
oh my friend..*

I disconnect all with the same..

Happiness said with a roar..

I am always a receiver..

*peace said softly..I am always an
observer..*

Which give decisions, the power..

There was silence for sometime..
between peace and happiness....
And the judgement was passed
by mind..which was fearless..

Outcome of happiness cannot be
peace but..outcome of peace is
always happiness..

and the mystery was resolved
without prejudice..
-Sampada

13. Revenge

Revenge

Revenge can be taken in a new
way..
by proving yourself..
you can leave no words to say..

there's no need to become a self
prey..
but only change the rules to play

take revenge for failure by
victory..
win your limitations with
opportunities..
beat your weakness by strength..
and convert your doubts into
beliefs
go away from fears of mysteries
and puzzles..

and remember..
revenge with self can create
miracles !!

-Sampada

14. दीपस्तंभ

दीपस्तंभ..

छोटा था.. तो पानी में तैर कर
दूर-दूर तक जाता था..
बड़ी-बड़ी लहरों से भी..
डर नहीं लगता था..
कुछ साल बाद, उन्ही लहरों पर
सवार होता था
पानी में गिरना भी अच्छा लगता था

फिर दौर ऐसा आया, कि फूलों से सजी
नाव में..
नशा सा लगता था
लाइफ जैकेट भी तब बेकार लगता था..
इसी लाइफ जैकेट पर बाद में..बच्चों
को लेक्चर देता था
छोटा बेटा पानी में गिरता था..तब लेकिन
डर लगता था
उसे तैरना सिखाने के लिए..
मैं खुद उसके साथ जाया करता था..
.. फिर समझा,की बड़ी-बड़ी लहरों को..
वह खुद झेलना चाहता था..

अब तक मैं इतनी लहरें और सागर..पार
करके आया था..

कि अब किनारे पर शांति से..बैठना
चाहता था..
अब एक जगह बैठ गया..तो भी कोई गम
नहीं था
.. बेटे ने कहा,
आपके आशीर्वाद का और अनुभव का
प्रकाश..
हमें तो मिलना ही था..

हमारा दीपस्तंभ तो.. आपको बना ही
था..
हमारा दीपस्तंभ तो.. आपको बना ही
था..
-संपदा

15. Feel Like a Queen..

Feel Like a Queen..

When the signal turns green..
Everything is paused...
only you are moving..
Then..you feel like a Queen..

When you enter home tired..
You find the home is tidy and
clean..
Then..you feel like a Queen..

When in heavy rain..
you are waiting for a bus..
and you see a friend in car.. is
crossing..
Then..you feel like a Queen..

Hours and hours of trekking..
and you see a blooming tree on
the skyline.
Then..you feel like a Queen..

You just woke up with a bad
dream..
and see in your phone...

Your Mom is online...
Then..you feel like a Queen..

After long hours of working..
if someone is waiting at home..
with a glass of wine...
Then..you feel like a Queen..

-Sampada

16. Change..the essence of life..

Change..the essence of life..

Change must happen..
this time-honored path..
must be embraced...
From the voice..that comes from
within..
Something must happen..that is
divine..
that divine will happen..we must
believe..

when the dark clouds of doubt..
began to gather,
we think..
why only me..who feels this
way?

But when the clouds pass..
and the sky is clear..
then lands up.. that confidence..

This is only me...who feels this
way !!!

-Sampada

17. Gift of seasons..

Gift of seasons..

Even in the blistering
summer..blossom just like a
flower..
even in deep anguish...be the
lighthouse for the other..

let the darkest mist..fade away..
of winters
and the bloom will make its
way..through fears.

the dry leaves of fall..will pave
the way for greens..
and the breeze of autumn..will
cool down the summers..
let the rain drops flow..in the
streams..
and rinse off...the stress n
worries of minds..

let the clouds melt again..
and get the silver linings..
let one season escort the other..
and bring us..gifts and
blessings..!!
-Sampada

18. नियम

नियम

रास्ते होते हैं हमारे लिए.. चलते तो रहना
ही है..
सबको मिलेगा मौका..आगे तो जाना ही
है

कार वाले भी चलाएंगे,
रिक्शा वाले भी चलाएंगे,
साइकिल वाले भी चलाएंगे..
आखिर मंजिल सब की एक ही है..

नियम और ध्यान दोनों जरूरी है..
हर एक जिंदगी कीमती जो है..

जहां मुड़ना है,वह निर्देश देना भी जरूरी
है..
बिना निर्देश दिए..नहीं तो.. अंतिम घड़ी
भी आ सकती है..

किसी की मां राह देख रही है..
किसी की बेटी राह देख रही है..

कोई घर पहुंचने की राह देख रहा है..
आखिर दिन भर की थकावट दूर जो
करनी है..

आपातकाल की स्थिति अगर है..
तो सुविधा मिलनी भी जरूरी है..
पल भर का इम्तिहान है..
उसी पल में लेकिन पहुंचना जरूरी है..

समय-समय की बात है..
परीक्षा अगर हो.. तो समय पर जाना
जरूरी है..

विधि और नियम का सम्मान और पालन
अगर है..
तो कोई भी रास्ता मुश्किल नहीं है..

आखिर सफर अच्छा हो..तो घर भी खुश
है..
घर खुश है तो शहर और देश भी खुश
है..

-संपदा

19. Sky of mind..

Sky of mind..

*Looked up through the window
grid one day..
and saw the bright.. blue sky of
May..*

*the sky was moving leisurely.. by
the bay..
with some spots and dots, just
like a spray..*

but..oh..dear, it was the window
grid.. looking that way..
But, one can see a shimmering
sky..
once the dust is blown away..

our mind is just like that sky of
May..
with the dark clouds..that we
portray..

the clouds of doubt..
the clouds of fear..
the clouds of ego..

the clouds of guilt..
that soak everyday..

just wonder...if all the dark
clouds meltdown one day..
once again..the sky of our mind
will sparkle brightly..by the bay !!

-Sampada

20. Expand your Horizon..

Expand your Horizon..

Expand your Horizon boundless..

go beyond the problems..that are countless..
and unfold the solutions which are flawless..

In a shrunken circle..even a tiny dot is visible..

in a sprawled circle though..it
will be invisible..

sometimes, stand in the shade of
a blooming green tree..
It's a promise,you will find
yourself worry free..

look at the huge mountain
sometimes..
you will learn to stay grounded
at all times..

lie down under the sky, glittering
with stars..

*It will show you the road, and
you will forget all the scars..*

*spend the sunset times on the
seashore..*
*the sea waves will take you to
your core..*

*take a dive in your infinite inner
world..*
*you will get answers,which are
still blurred..*

-Sampada

21. A perfect chord

A perfect chord

When I wish to express
deep..from my heart..
no words or alphabets..give me a
perfect start

It is the sacred language of
music..that plays an important
part..

It may take any form..

a note.. a beat.. a string.. or a
chord..

The hard beats of drums..
fire up the spirits..
the high, brassy notes of a
trumpet..
witness a victory to celebrate..

the tender.. streaming notes of a
violin..
lighten our heart..
we relish in our own sphere..
when the striking strings of
guitar,we hear..

The empty spaces in the flute..
take our hearts..
to the root
The ringing bells remind us..
the twinkling of stars..

The blowing of conch shells..
connect us to the Lord..

when words fail..
music strikes a perfect chord..
music strikes a perfect chord..

-Sampada